HOW TO CARE FOR YOUR NEW PET

CARING FOR
MY NEW
GERBIL

John Bankston

Mitchell Lane
PUBLISHERS

2001 SW 31st Avenue
Hallandale, FL 33009
www.mitchelllane.com

First Edition, 2019.

Author: John Bankston
Designer: Ed Morgan
Editor: Sharon F. Doorasamy

Names/credits:
Title: Caring for My New Gerbil / by John Bankston
Description: Hallandale, FL : Mitchell Lane Publishers, [2019]

Series: How to Care for Your New Pet

Library bound ISBN: 9781680203240

eBook ISBN: 9781680203257

Photo credits: Design elements and photos Freepik.com/Getty Images, cover photos Robert Owen-Wahl freeimages.com, p. 4-5 koki lino/Getty Images, p. 6-7 Jane Burton/Getty Images, p. 8-9 Svetlanistaya/Getty Images, p. 10-11 Alicia Lohnes/Eyeem/ Getty Images, p. 12-13 Max Bailen/Getty Images, p. 14-15 Frank Greenaway, p. 16-17 CamilioTorres/Getty Images, p. 18-19 Kerrick/ Getty Images, p. 20-21 Arco Christine/Getty Images, p. 22-23 Zsv3207/Getty Images, p. 24-25 MediaProduction/Getty Images, p. 26 Robert Owen-Wahl, p. 29 Robert Owen-Wahl

CONTENTS

Words in **bold** throughout can be found in the Glossary.

Gerbil World

Before the 1950s, there were no pet gerbils in the United States. Wild gerbils lived in Asia and Africa. They might have stayed there. Then in 1954, Dr. Victor Schwentker ordered 11 pairs of Mongolian gerbils for his lab. He quickly learned what gerbils do best—make more gerbils. His lab was overrun. He began giving them to friends.

Today gerbils are popular pets. They rarely bite. They are easy to care for. They don't take up much space. They are clean and don't smell bad. An exercise wheel in their cage gives them plenty to do.

Gerbils are also friendly and curious. They enjoy walking on the hands or laps of their owners. And like potato chips, you can't have just one.

DID YOU KNOW?

Mongolia is a country between Russia and China. It is best known as the home of the fearsome warrior Genghis Khan. In the early 1200s, he ruled over the largest connected land empire in history.

Gerbil Facts

Gerbils are rodents. This means they are related to mice, rats, and hamsters. The largest rodent in North America is the beaver. Like other rodents, gerbils have very strong teeth which never stop growing.

Gerbils are the kangaroo of the rodent world. Like that Australian animal, gerbils' back legs are longer then their front ones. This makes them great jumpers. It also makes them skilled escape artists. Many gerbil owners are surprised by how easily they get out of a secure cage.

Of course, the Mongolian gerbil is not the only type. It belongs to a **subspecies** that includes jirds and sand rats. There are more than 100 different kinds.

The great gerbil from Turkmenistan in Central Asia can be more than one foot long. Mongolian gerbils are much smaller. Their bodies are about four inches long. Their tails are the same length as their bodies. The tails have a little tuft of fur.

Most Mongolian gerbils are light brown with creamy or gray bellies. However, **breeders** have produced a wide variety of colors including yellow, spotted, and gray. Gerbils sit up. They do this when they eat, holding food in their front paws. They also sit up to drink from a water bottle. Mostly they seem to enjoy watching us as we watch them.

DID YOU KNOW?
The Indian gerbil can leap 15 feet.

Get Ready

Moving to a new place can be scary. If you've ever moved, you know how hard it can be. It can be even harder for a gerbil. When you bring it home, it might be scared. You want it to feel safe. To do that, you have to prepare.

The stores selling gerbils also sell their supplies. Don't get both at the same time. Instead, get your gerbil supplies first. You don't want your gerbil waiting. That would be like living in a moving van while they built your house!

Before you shop, pick out the place your gerbil can call home. A desktop, a table, or a bookcase can work. The space should be about two feet long and one foot wide.

Remember Goldilocks? Your new gerbil will be like her. You don't want a space that is too hot. You need an area away from direct sunlight. You don't want its home near a heating vent.

You also don't want a space that is too cold.

If there is a draft blowing under your door, make sure it's away from your gerbil's new home. This is why it should be a few feet up.

Take the time to clear off the surface. Then you will be ready to get a gerbil house.

Setting up the Gerbilarium

There are lots of choices for your gerbil's new home. There are metal cages and plastic cages. Experts say you should get a **gerbilarium**. This is an aquarium for gerbils.

Gerbils are different from hamsters or mice. Their home needs to be different too. Putting a gerbil in a cage built for a mouse will make it unhappy. Gerbils don't need fake tunnels. They build their own.

Gerbils like to use their teeth. Those teeth are very strong. They often tear off pieces of plastic cages.

Sometimes they swallow the plastic. This can make them very sick.

With metal cages, gerbils can hurt their teeth. Their feet can get stuck in the mesh. If there is enough space they can even shimmy out. Gerbils can squirm through a hole less then one inch square. Plus, they will push paper and other bits through the mesh. This can be very messy.

Gerbilariums are ideal. They offer a flat surface. There is nothing for them to chew on. Plus, they won't be able to climb up the sides and escape.

The one bad thing is they get hot. That's why you don't want them right by a window where the sun will be shining. You want to have a wire cage over the top. This protects the gerbil. It lets them breathe. It also keeps them from escaping.

Have an adult help you set up the gerbilarium. Because they are fairly heavy and made of glass, you shouldn't try to move them alone.

On the bottom of the gerbilariums add a layer of organic soil or peat. On top of that, add a layer of hay.

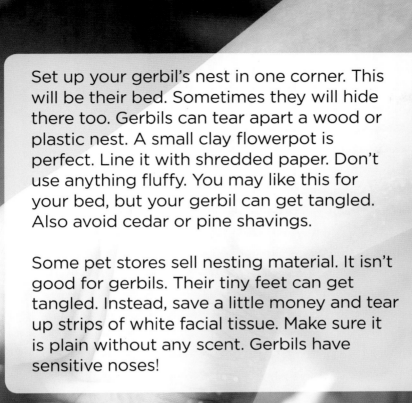

Set up your gerbil's nest in one corner. This will be their bed. Sometimes they will hide there too. Gerbils can tear apart a wood or plastic nest. A small clay flowerpot is perfect. Line it with shredded paper. Don't use anything fluffy. You may like this for your bed, but your gerbil can get tangled. Also avoid cedar or pine shavings.

Some pet stores sell nesting material. It isn't good for gerbils. Their tiny feet can get tangled. Instead, save a little money and tear up strips of white facial tissue. Make sure it is plain without any scent. Gerbils have sensitive noses!

Near their nest, you can place their bathtub. You won't be filling it with water. Gerbils don't get clean that way. They like dust! In the desert, rolling around in the sand gets rid of **moisture** on their skin. In their new home, they will love rolling around in **chinchilla** sand.

A small, ceramic bowl is perfect for feeding. They easily tip over lighter bowls. Use a small bowl. If you use a big bowl, you might fill it up and overfeed them. If you have two gerbils living together, don't put all their food in one bowl. Scatter it around their home. This will keep them foraging instead of fighting.

Hang a metal or glass water bottle on one side of the cage. This should be a special bottle made for gerbils. It has a stopper so it doesn't drip out. Keep it high enough so it doesn't spill onto their bedding.

Everything you've added must be changed regularly. The aquarium should be washed once a week. Make sure you rinse out any liquid soap you use.

Your gerbils will also need fresh sand and water every day. It's up to you to keep the gerbilarium clean. No matter how often you ask, your gerbil won't do it.

DID YOU KNOW?

Pet gerbils are illegal in California. Agriculture officials worry that gerbils will escape or be released by their owners, and do a lot of damage to crops there.

Getting Gerbil

Gerbils aren't just easy to care for. They are easy to buy as well.

If you know a friend with a gerbil, they can tell you where they got them. Or maybe their gerbil is about to have baby gerbils. They need to stay with their mother for several weeks. After that, you can take two home.

You may have thought the only place to buy a gerbil was at the pet store. Many animal shelters take in smaller animals, such as rabbits, hamsters, and gerbils. Have an adult in your house help with the search. You may find pictures online.

Breeders raise gerbils. They may cost more than at the store. It can be worth it. They usually tame their gerbils. That means your new pet will be happy to climb into the palm of your hand.

Take the time to carefully look at your new friend. It shouldn't be squinting. Its fur should be soft, not rough. It should have lots of energy and get along with the other gerbils in its home.

It is not a good idea to buy a gerbil from a stranger. Gerbils can have fleas. Some are sick. People can get sick from gerbils. This is one reason you want to wash your hands before and after playing with a gerbil.

Gerbils are **social**. That means they won't be happy living alone. Pairs of gerbils live longer than solo gerbils. Your best bet will be to bring home gerbils that already know each other. Make sure to get two boys or two girls. Otherwise you could have a lot of gerbils.

DID YOU KNOW?
An adult female gerbil can have 4–10 babies every 24 days.

Bringing Gerbil Home

When you've chosen a gerbil or two, you can take them home in a critter keeper. This is a small plastic **carrier** with a handle. Put an inch of bedding in the bottom. Add a little food in the middle.

To keep your gerbils happy and busy on the ride home, give them a toilet paper tube.

When you get home, introduce your gerbils to their gerbilarium. Set their critter carrier inside and open it so they can get out. Then leave them alone. You shouldn't pick them up or play with them their first day. Let them get used to their new home.

If your gerbils aren't already friends, they should be kept separate. A wire screen can be placed in the middle of their gerbilarium. Put one gerbil on either side. This lets them get used to each other.

Gerbils can be fun and social. Still, you need to be gentle. The key to getting them to accept you is to accept your hand. Place your hand inside their home. You can even put food in it. If they nibble on your hand, don't yell. Just say "no" in a firm voice. You can also blow on them. This will teach them not to bite you.

It will take a few days of training before they will let you pick them up. Gerbils can be squirmy. Some are shy.

When the gerbil has gotten used to your hand, place it around its body. Your hand should be just behind its front legs. Support its bottom with your other hand. Never, ever pick it up by its tail. This can hurt it.

Be gentle. Don't squeeze it.

You can use the carrier to bring it to a safe, enclosed space. An empty bathtub can be a good place to play. Sit with them and they will start to climb over you.

Be very careful of other pets. Keep cats, dogs, and snakes away from your gerbil. If you have younger brothers or sisters, watch them as well.

Eat Like a Gerbil

Have you ever been told to eat more fruits and vegetables? Well, no one has to tell your gerbil. That's pretty much all they eat.

Wild gerbils are **foragers**. They eat things such as grass, seeds, or leaves.

Your pet should eat special gerbil pellets. They only need a tablespoon a day. They will be so happy if you also give them treats.

Have an adult in your house slice up a few pieces of apples or carrots. Offer your new friend a few pieces of broccoli. Other foods they enjoy include cucumbers and pumpkin.

DO NOT FEED YOUR GERBIL:

Potatoes (including french fries or tater tots), rhubarb, or the leaves from a tomato. They are **poisonous.** Grapes or raisins are also bad. These foods can make a gerbil very sick.

They also love melons, like cantaloupe. Or you can give them a piece of an orange. Be careful with these fruits. Just give them a little. The sugar in fruit can make a gerbil sick.

Gerbils are very curious. They will try just about anything once.

Gerbil Tricks

Gerbils love to dig. In their desert home, they burrow deep tunnels. Inside their underground home, each gerbil can store almost one-pound of food.

Let your new friend follow its **instincts**. Bury food around its nest. Then watch it dig.

The exercise wheel is an important part of every gerbil home. Your wheel should be solid. Mesh wheels can trap its feet. Some owners buy a hamster wheel and then put tape over its mesh. That way its tail won't get stuck.

Other things they enjoy playing with include thick wood, ladders, ramps, and platforms. Be careful with anything that can fall and hurt your gerbil. If you use a rock for playtime, it should have a flat bottom so it doesn't tip.

Gerbils love toilet paper tubes. Set a tube down beside them. They will usually squirm in and out a few times. Then they will tear them up. They can usually tear a toilet paper tube apart in about five minutes. Gerbils are great paper shredders.

DID YOU KNOW?

In labs, rats and mice are taught to run mazes. Gerbils refuse.

Visiting the Vet

A few days after bringing your gerbil home, you'll need to take it to a **veterinarian**. This is a special doctor that only treats animals. If you have another pet, their vet can also treat your gerbil. The place where you got your gerbil should also know the name of a good veterinarian.

After the first visit, you should take your gerbil to the vet every six months. If your gerbil stops eating or doesn't have any energy, you should take it to the vet right away. Pay attention if your gerbil seems to have trouble breathing. If it starts sneezing a lot, that's another sign it needs to see a vet.

Besides an exam to make sure your new gerbil is healthy and happy, the vet will check it for fleas and lice. You may have questions about caring for your gerbil. The vet is a great person to ask.

DID YOU KNOW?

Some scientists now believe gerbils and not rats were responsible for a deadly plague that killed millions in Europe in the 1200s. The plague started from fleas carried on the gerbil's bodies.

Gerbil Speak

Watch your gerbils. When they say hi, they kiss. They touch their mouths together. Their **saliva** helps them recognize each other.

When a gerbil stands and puts its front paws together it isn't praying. It's worried. When they stand with their paws apart, they are curious. As you get to know your gerbils, you will learn how they behave. They will probably learn about you too!

SHOPPING LIST

When you are ready to bring home a gerbil, have an adult take you to your local pet store. This is a list of some things you will need:

- [ ] A gerbilarium—an aquarium that's at least 10 gallons with a well-fitting mesh cover

- [ ] Bedding and nesting material

- [ ] Nesting box

- [ ] Water bottle and holder

- [ ] Food dish

- [ ] Gerbil chow

- [ ] Exercise wheel

- [ ] Sand bath

- [ ] Toys

- [ ] Treats

- [ ] A critter keeper to bring them home

FIND OUT MORE

Online

There are a number of sites that will help you raise a healthy and happy gerbil.

To learn about gerbil care:

http://www.twinsqueaks.com

The Humane Society offers advice and can connect you with shelters near you where you can adopt gerbils:

http://m.humanesociety.org/animals/gerbils/tips/welcoming_new_gerbils.html?credit=web_id81798438

http://m.humanesociety.org/animals/gerbils/tips/gerbils_as_pets.html?credit=web_id81798438

http://m.humanesociety.org/animals/gerbils/tips/gerbil_housing.html?credit=web_id81798438

Pet names: Here's a fun site to find a great pet name.

https://www.bowwow.com.au

Books

Black, Vanessa. *Gerbils*. Minneapolis, MN: Jump!, Inc. 2017

Thomas, Isabel. *Giggle's Guide to Caring for Your Gerbils*. Chicago, IL: Heinemann Library, 2015.

GLOSSARY

breeders
Someone who mates animals to produce offsprings

carrier
Safe container to transport an animal

chinchilla
A small mammal with very soft fur from the mountains of South America

foragers
An animal that digs and searches for food

gerbilarium
An aquarium for gerbils

instincts
An inner force that causes an animal to act in a certain way

moisture
A small amount of water or other liquid that forms on something

poisonous
Substance that is dangerous or deadly

saliva
Spit

social
Comfortable playing and being around others

subspecies
A particular type within a species

veterinarian
An animal doctor

BIBLIOGRAPHY

Alexander, Bryan. "Lost characters of 'Zootopia' found." *USA Today*, June 6, 2016.

"Gerbil Care Guide." VetBabble. https://www.vetbabble.com/small-pets/gerbil-care/.

Hicks, Ritchie. "9 Things to Consider When Buying a Gerbil." Pethelpful, April 8, 2017. https://pethelpful.com/rodents/9-Things-To-Consider-when-Buying-a-Gerbil.

Kranking, Kathy W., and Alton Langford. "No way! I can't be a gerbil!" *Ranger Rick*, January 1996.

McLeod, Dr. Lianne. "Guide to Gerbils as Pets." *The Spruce Pets*, October 11, 2017. https://www.thesprucepets.com/mongolian-gerbils-as-pets-1236822.

Mullen, Jethro. "Plague blame game: Gerbils replace rats as prime suspects." CNN Wire, February 25, 2015.

Perry, Diane. "The gnawing issue." *Boy's Quest*, June-July 2012.

Sneed, Dani. "Gerbils morphing." *Highlights for Children*, May 2003.

INDEX

ABOUT THE AUTHOR

John Bankston
The author of more than 100 books for young readers, John Bankston lives in Miami Beach, Florida, with his ChiJack rescue dog named Astronaut.